# A Cowboy Spirit

# A Cowboy Spirit

Stuart Hooker

| Library of Congress Control Number: | | 2013913430 |
| --- | --- | --- |
| ISBN: | Hardcover | 978-1-4836-7265-6 |
| | Softcover | 978-1-4836-7264-9 |
| | Ebook | 978-1-4836-7266-3 |

This book was printed in the United States of America.

Rev. date: 07/26/2013

**To order additional copies of this book, contact:**
Xlibris LLC
1-888-795-4274
www.Xlibris.com
Orders@Xlibris.com
138816

# Contents

# Cowboy Spirit

There's a cowboy rode down this trail a hundred years ago,
A century now, his tracks have been gone,
I drive these cows the way he did, 'though his thoughts I cannot know,
But I know his spirit lingers on;

It lingers in the valley where he built his corral,
It lingers near the mound of dirt where he dug his well,
It lingers on the trail that switchbacks up the mountainside,
It lingers everywhere he used to ride;

I feel his spirit with me when I step out at night,
When I light up a smoke and watch the sky,
I feel his spirit near me sayin,' "Everything's all right,"
"As long as cowboys give it their best try;"

It lingers in his old cabin where we now store the grain,
It lingers ever' time it starts to rain,
It lingers near the shade tree, while I tack on a shoe,
It lingers on the gather where he's part of the crew;

I feel him often urgin' me to do a little more,
To be the best cowboy I can be,
And I'm grateful to the cowboy who rode these trails before,
I feel his spirit lingerin' near to me;

It lingers in the tack room where ancient saddles rest,
It lingers 'cross the ranges of the west,
It lingers 'mong the mesquites and the oak brush on the hill,
It lingers here and it always will;

# Ever Seen A Cowboy

Have you ever seen a cowboy on a windswept ridge alone,
Starin' across the country like he's chiseled there in stone,
His horse standin' beside him, ears up, he's lookin,' too,
And way off, in the distance, are the mountains far and blue;

Have you ever wrangled horses in the dim pre-light of dawn,
Smelled woodsmoke from the cabin where there's hot, black coffee on,
Have you climbed into the saddle with your fingers stiff and cold,
Then felt your sorrel hump up so you took a real good hold;

Have you ever roped a "big 'un" when no one knew where you were at,
Then had to go back lookin' for your "stompled," trompled hat,
Have you ever heard the wisdom in an old hand's tales,
Then had to run from a mad old cow when that wisdom fails;

Have you ever wished for a faster horse, or at least a slower steer,
Have you looked back up the trail and wondered "can I get out of here,"
Have you ever seen a bad old cow guard her sickly calf,
Or watched a youngster smile 'cause he made an old hand laugh;

Have you ever seen a cowgirl when she brought a wild one in,
Or heard her daddy proudly say, "She did it again,"
Have you ever seen a dust cloud boil behind a herd of steers,
Or seen a rancher smile at the first "good" rain in years;

Have you ever stood in a dry corral with so many calves to brand,
That you couldn't see how you'd get it done, then a kid makes a hand,
Have you ever tracked a wild cow wonderin' who's gonna find who first,
Or drank from a murky dirt tank 'cause you had to quench your thirst;

Have you ridden back to cow camp after you turned the cattle out,
Knowin' you've done a good job, that's what cowboyin's about,
Have you sat outside the bunkhouse after all the chores were done,
Thinkin' the roan did good today, watchin' the settin' sun;

Have you ever seen a cowboy on a windswept ridge alone,
Starin' across the country like he's chiseled there in stone,
If so, well we've been blessed, my friend, to know the cowboy ways,
I've seen that cowboy on that ridge, I've helped him gather strays.

I rode my horse to the windmill at Nine Mile,
An old man gettin' a drink there got a big smile,
He said, "I talked to someone, but it's been a while,"
"Can you stop and talk a spell with me at Nine Mile;"

I let my grulla drink as I filled my canteen,
That was the loneliest man I think I've ever seen,
I rolled me a smoke then tossed him my sack,
He said, "If you got extry, I'll trade some hard tack;"

I told him to keep the sack, I had more in my gear,
Then asked him how he come to be way out here,
He said him and his mule were just passin' through,
Some of the loneliest country he ever knew;

See, he'd been a business man in San Francisco,
When his wife and child died he decided he'd go,
Disappear in the back country all alone,
Where God had showed him things no one has known;

He pulled his Bible out, so worn and tattered,
Said, "It's written here, all that ever mattered,"
"Seems most folks don't care 'less somethin' helps them,"
"So, I talk to my mule, myself, and to Him;"

I gave him what I could then said, "Goodbye,"
He said to ride with God, I told him I'd try,
At the bunkhouse with my Good Book, I have to smile,
Seems I found inspiration out at Nine Mile.

# All My Cowboys Were Girls

I didn't think about it when we saddled up that day,
Tammy rode her palomino, I picked out my bay,
Sandra caught her dun, Holly had the roan whose mane has curls,
I never thought about it, but all my cowboys were girls;

We piled into the four-door, the trailer was loaded down,
We stopped to get some diesel, as we drove through town,
The only station open was that run-down place of Earl's,
It still hadn't hit me that all my cowboys were girls;

By noon we had 'em gathered then took a break for lunch,
We's laughin' and relaxin,' that was sure a topnotch bunch,
After brandin,' headin' home, listenin' to a song of Merle's,
Holly laughed and said, "Grandpa, all your cowboys are girls;"

It shocked me when I heard it, then I laughed out loud,
The way they worked them cattle would make my grandpa proud,
I had to quote a great cowgirl when we cleared a cattleguard,
"To cowboy up is easy, but to 'Cowgirl Up,' that's hard;"

I've rode with lots of cowboys and lots of cowgirls too,
It's never about gender when there's work to do,
I've learned a bit of wisdom, through life I've heard some pearls,
"Don't judge someone 'til you've been down that trail, some of the best
    cowboys are girls."

# Team Ropers From Hell

We's pushin' cattle 'cross a mesa in New Mexico,
When thunder clouds built up fast, boss said, "Boys, we've got to go,"
We aimed them cows down country as thunder shook the air,
They's a rocky canyon down below and we had to get 'em there;

The rain started comin' hard as lightnin' filled the sky,
We all donned our slickers but it was too late to stay dry,
Them cattle started off the mesa, but they moved awful slow,
'Cept for two horned yearlin' bulls that took off way down below;

I knew we couldn't lose 'em, so I took down my rope,
And headed off that mesa at a fearsome lope,
As I went by Ol' Charlie, he yelled, "I've got your back,"
Then passin' a big old rocky bluff, I felt the lightnin' crack;

The flash, at first it blinded me, then I could see all right,
And to my dyin' day I won't forget that wretched sight,
Two cowboys, all dressed in black, seemed to come out of the rock,
I just stared at 'em speechless, I's way too scared to talk;

They's ridin' two black geldings whose eyes looked all ablaze,
Around 'em was a glowin' yellow, kinda fiery haze,
Each had a shiny rope circlin' up above his head,
And if I didn't know better, I'd a' said, "Them guys look dead;"

But we was chasin' yearlin's so I gigged that big bay, hard,
I heard hoofbeats behind me, I knew that's my pard,
Well, I lined out a yearlin' bull, but I roped him 'round the neck,
I seen them other cowboys and they nearly had a wreck;

Then their header got one side and then the other horn,
But Ol' Charlie's the best heeler I've seen since I was born,
So when I turned that yearlin' bull, I knew just how "Right" feels,
Then I swung my bay around, Charlie had 'im by two heels;

The bull went down, I threw my rope, I had to get two feet tied,
That other header was on his bull, them cowboys could ride,
They beat us by full seconds, then I don't know where they went,
Ol' Charlie just set there gapin,' he said, "They left, hell bent;"

I took my rope off our bull, we had them yearlin's hobbled,
I felt we could a' took 'em if I just hadn't bobbled,
When the trail boss got to us, he said, "You boys did well,"
We'd decided not to talk about those Team Ropers From Hell.

# Crossin' the Gila

We had to cross the Gila on that muggy summer day,
Rains brought the flood that took the drift fences away,
The cattle were balled up on the east side river bank,
When I saw that muddy flood, that's when my heart sank;

See, I never learned to swim, I'd sink like a rock,
When it came time to dive in, I let my horse balk,
Brother rode up beside me and yelled, "Do what I do,"
He gigged his palomino and through the air they flew;

When he splashed in the water, I's already in the air,
My horse's head went under, I thought we'd die right there,
Brother yelled, "Now slide back, hang on like I am,"
My horses' head came up, we's out of a jamb;

Then we started laughin' like we'd never laughed before,
'Though muddy river water filled our every pore,
He said, "Never mind the cattle when you reach the other side,"
"Climb back in your saddle, that's the time to ride;"

When I's back in my saddle I heard brother shout,
"Trade me ropes, I'll catch another, you pull this calf out,"
"But watch out for his mama, she's mad as can be,"
"If you need help to cut 'im loose, just wait for me;"

I'd seen this done before so I worked on my slack,
The calf was with his mama, when brother came ridin' back,
I told him, "That was fun, but let's not cross a flood again,"
He asked me how I's gettin' home, then he began to grin.

# Knew A Cowboy

Knew a cowboy
had three horses in his string,
He had two dinks
and one 'could do most anything,
So he rode that good horse ever' day
them dinks just once or twice,
And ridin' on that good horse, well,
the days went awful nice,
'Til that good horse got so wore out
that he finally came down sick,
So he "babied" and he "doctored" him
he hoped it'd do the trick;

Knew a cowboy
had three horses in his string,
He had two dinks
and one 'could do most anything,
He rode them dinks most ever' day
as the good horse got his rest,
Them dinks improved in ever' way
and the cowboy, he confessed,
I done my good horse wrong, I know
but he's all better now,
Them dinks improved and how they've growed
they've learned to watch a cow;

Knew a cowboy
had three horses in his string,
He had two dinks
and one 'could do most anything . . .

# The Boss's Saddle

It was winter-time and it was cold,
That fencin' job was gettin' old,
I put the tools back in the truck,
Drove to the ranch and just my luck;

The other hand was late, again,
I opened the gate, let the horses in,
I put out hay to the horses and cattle,
Then stopped to look at the boss's saddle;

It was carved with acorns and leaves of oak,
I'd get one like that, 'cept I was broke,
See, a workin' man don't make a lot,
But he takes pride in what he's got;

A friend said, once when we's in a drouth,
I's born with a silver spoon in my mouth,
I's the only one he ever knew about,
That took that spoon and spit it out;

Well, I was raised on our family ranch,
I was in line, on the workin' branch,
But Grandpa died 'fore he got it all set,
They split that ranch and we're fightin,' yet;

So, I'm off workin' for another man,
And it's hard to pay for a good top hand,
As ranchers go, this one's top-notch,
Like a good calf horse, he doesn't scotch;

But I'm not gettin' ahead this way,
I'll go find somethin' else some day,
I've got to settle in and work right now,
Aw, get outta the tack room, you danged old cow.

# I've Outlived Lots of Horses

I've outlived lots of horses, I've had good ones from the start,
I've outlived lots of horses, but they live on in my heart,
I've outlived lots of horses, I rode each one with pride,
I've outlived lots of horses, broke my heart when each one died;

You cain't help but love horses, each one's different than the rest,
You cain't help but love horses, hard to say which one's the best,
One may be good in mountains, one may have a lot more speed,
All of them have somethin' that a cowboy may need;

I guess my best horse is the one I'm ridin' now,
He's got lots of bottom, and he understands a cow,
Sometimes he puts up with them, like he puts up with me,
But, when I'm on him, ridin,' he sets my soul plumb free;

You know what I'm sayin,' a horse can get your heart,
Even if he bucked you off when you thought you's so smart,
He ain't a pet, he ain't a tool, the relationship is strange,
Between a cowboy and his horse, out workin' on the range;

I've outlived lots of horses, I've had good ones from the start,
I've outlived lots of horses, but they live on in my heart,
I've outlived lots of horses, I rode each one with pride,
I've outlived lots of horses, broke my heart when each one died.

# He's At the End Of His Rope

Two ropers, two sets of flankers and soon we'll get this job done,
But tyin' the big one they're draggin' to us may not be a whole lot of fun,
He's strugglin' and bellerin,' tryin' to get loose, that calf's plumb
    full of hope,
Truth is, that calf will get branded today see, he's at the end of his rope;

He'll fight, he'll kick, he'll try to get up soon he'll be down and tied tight,
This mornin' he's in the "unbranded count" he'll be a "steer calf" tonight,
He'll never give up and lay still for us, he shows us his answer is "nope,"
We'll struggle then we'll get 'im down, see, he's at the end of his rope;

I have to admire the fight in that calf to stay young, wild, and free,
I have to say that fightin' calf reminds me, somewhat, of me,
I've been in spots I shouldn't have been sometimes you just have to cope,
He's facin' a change he doesn't want, see, he's at the end of his rope;

Lyin' there, tied, he calls to his mama, from the herd you hear mama bawl,
Soon it's time to untie that calf, after he's been through it all,
He's up, he's headed back to his mama, tryin' a staggerin' lope,
'Cross the pen a roper drags up another, yep, he's at the end of his rope;

# Our Saddles Were Straight

We lined out up the trail like a train on a track,
Trail boss in the lead, a good hand in the back,
Climbed out a long ridge plumb to the top,
Trail boss, he pulled up, we all come to a stop;

Stepped down, readjusted and tightened our cinches,
With them horses warmed up, not a one even flinches,
Climbed back in our saddles, quiet as could be,
Spread out by the boss where we could all see;

"No tellin' what you'll find down there at the spring,"
"Take Rex with ya, and bring everything,"
"Hold 'em all up at the Head of Cottonwood,"
"You'll be the first there if your gather goes good;"

He lined out the others on their circles that day,
Then we all split up to go on our way,
We's ready for whatever would be brought by fate,
Our horses had rested, our saddles were straight.

# Another Hundred Years

A cowboy drove some cattle around a mountain side,
Spotted somethin' shiny, got down to see what he'd spied,
The cattle moved on along, by their own accord,
Covered by rocks, leaves, and time was an old cavalry sword;

Excited by the find, he thought he'd keep the blade,
A soldier must a'dropped it chasin' outlaws on a raid,
He quickly looked around hopin' for somethin' more,
Soon he found a brass button, like the cavalry soldiers wore;

He found some rusted metal like an old Colt Dragoon,
And other bits of history, the story came clear soon,
There were arrowheads, bits of saddles, and buttons everywhere,
Realizin' there'd been a great battle, the cowboy said a prayer;

He put back his trophies to the ground where they belong,
Stuck that saber in the ground, hung a US buckle on it's prong,
Them cattle looked kinda misty over his horse's ears,
He hopes another cowboy says another prayer,
in another hundred years.

# Night Herd

There's a half-moon shinin' so I can see a bit,
Though I don't like night herdin,' I know I'll never quit,
Workin' for some rancher, carin' for his cattle,
Miles away from town spendin' hours in the saddle;

(chorus)
There's a fire up near the wagon where the boys are gathered 'round,
'Fore they crawl in their bedrolls scattered on the ground,
I hear 'em softly laughin' but I can't make out a word,
'Cause I'm out in the darkness keepin' watch on night herd;

I picked out my grulla 'cause he sees good at night,
Slim's a-circlin' to the left, I move out to the right,
We moved them cows off water to where we've held 'em up,
There's coffee at the fire if we really need a cup;

A big old brindle steer gets up, some yearlin's follow suit,
As I ease out around 'em, an owl lets out a hoot,
I let 'em hear me comin' so they won't all run off,
Slim has seen 'em movin' too, I hear 'im softly cough;

The cattle graze a little while then they bed back down,
Later my relief shows up, wearin' a sleepy frown,
Slim and I slip back to camp as quiet as can be,
Glad we're done night herdin,' it ain't our cup a' tea;

# The Dog Is Smellin' My Saddle

The dog is smellin' my saddle,
He smells horses of long ago,
Back when I's workin' cattle,
Down in New Mexico;

I wonder if he smells old Dusty,
I wonder, does he smell the grey,
Even though my memory's rusty,
I'll bet he smells Dads' big bay;

I wonder if he can tell,
My sorrel from my line-back dun,
Or is it that bull he smells,
That I heeled at a flat-out run;

I wonder if he smells the campfire,
That I built at the head of Stone,
With snow pilin' up, higher and higher,
And I was cold plumb to the bone;

I wonder if he smells my fear,
From when that horse fell off a bluff with Dad,
Or when a rifle went off behind me,
The worst deer hunt we ever had;

Now he's lookin' back up at me,
I wonder what scent he caught,
From days in that saddle, ridin' free,
Makin' memories too soon forgot.

# Hell's Half-Acre

I don't know what was in the mind of The Maker,
When He created "Hell's Half-Acre,"
It's a jumbled up mess of bluffs and rock,
You ride through quiet, too amazed to talk;

There's places here where cattle won't go,
On solid rock where grass won't grow,
We trailed lions here, behind the hounds,
One trail just goes 'round and 'round;

You stop on a bluff where forty yards away,
To get there takes 'bout a half a day,
You ride mighty careful when you're up here,
You're on the edge feelin' wonder, and fear,

If old bay's shoe slips on the stone,
You'n be down, hurt, and all alone,
Had an uncle died like that in the past,
Wonder what he thought of there at the last;

I'm sure he thought of the life he'd had,
Of his mother, his sister, his brothers, his dad,
Of his little paint horse, his pride and joy,
So ride mighty careful through here, cowboy;

My grandparents homesteaded here years ago,
Where YL Canyon meets Bear Creek below,
The trees, like family, put roots in this ground,
Those roots, like old bay, are strong and sound;

Ride easy, good advice for any cowhand,
I feel there's angels watchin' over this land,
Hell's Half-Acre will be here long after I'm gone,
Maybe I'll see an angel, and the little paint he's on.

# Cowboy Is My Name

I've written lots of poems 'bout the cowboy life I've led,
The troubles I've encountered, the memories in my head,
I'd like to recite them in front of an interested crowd,
But my dentures just don't fit me, and I don't talk that loud;

But if they did and I could speak I wouldn't dress that garish,
I'd just be there to pass along some memories that I cherish,
I wouldn't wear no handkerchief tied around my throat,
I wouldn't wear no shaps made from some long dead goat;

I wouldn't wear my spurs in there, they's no need for that,
'Guess in an auditorium, it's okay to wear my hat,
I wouldn't try to fool no one, but I might make up a tale,
And I surely wouldn't tell them that I'd been in a jail;

I might tell 'em of some team ropers that don't exist nowhere,
Surely, they wouldn't believe me, I'd tell that tale with care,
I'd sure tell 'em some stories, most of which are true,
Mostly, I wouldn't stretch the truth like Hollywood writers do;

I'd wear my trusty denim jeans, my boots might be some worn,
That's mostly what I've always had, since the day I's born,
I'd tell my tales of workin' cows, no two tales quite the same,
And that's just how I'd do it, sure as Cowboy is my name.

# Grandpa's Boots

Grandpa's boots were worn and muddy
so he'd leave them outside,
Which was good 'cause Granny's cats needed
another good place to hide,
Their cousins, the barn cats sat watchin'
Grandpa milk the cow,
He'd hit 'em all with one stream of milk
'though I still don't know how;

Where have all the good times gone
fond memories of growin' up,
Helpin' Grandpa shuck the corn on
the tailgate of his old truck,
He'd kneel so I'd step from his knee
to the stirrup on a gentle horse,
He had one suit he'd wear to town
and Sundays to church, of course;

He left us great footprints to follow
sometimes too big to fill,
Though he's been gone so many years
in my mind I see him still,
And his boots so worn and muddy
that he'd leave them outside,
Which was good 'cause Granny's cats needed
another good place to hide.

# It's Snowin' In the Rockies Tonight

She called me up from Phoenix, she said, "I hope you're all right,"
"I know you're working cattle, I'll bet your world is white,"
I said, "Yeah, it's been snowin' and the cold winds sure can blow,"
"But thoughts of you keep me warm, and Baby, you should know;"

(chorus:)
The cattle works are 'bout over, what a time we've had,
It's cold and lonely here, girl, I sure miss you bad,
Soon I'll come over, you will be such a sight,
You're in my thoughts and heart, girl, and it's snowin' in the Rockies, tonight;

She said, "I'll finish college, I graduate in May,"
I said, "I'll be there for you nothing can keep me away,"
She said, "Honey, be careful, Christmas break's in a few more weeks,"
"And keep out of the driftin' snow, up on those mountain peaks;"

(repeat chorus)

We found this song he'd been writin' in the pocket of his coat,
We mailed it to her in Phoenix, the last words her cowboy wrote,
See, his horse took a fall off a rimrock wall, her cowboy's last ride,
He's all alone, when the Lord took him home, and into the cold wind
       he cried:

(final chorus:)
The cattle works are 'bout over, what a time we've had,
It's cold and lonely here, girl, I sure miss you bad,
Looks like I won't be over, I know you're a beautiful sight,
You're in my thoughts and heart, girl, and it's snowin' in the Rockies tonight.

# The Team Roper

He rode into the arena on his great big bay,
A girl by the rail said, "I'll marry him someday,"
Don't think he didn't see her, he even tried to flirt,
But when he threw that heel loop, he caught nothin' but dirt;

You should ride, Cowboy, ride,
Swing your loop far and wide,
Head to the sunset with all your pride,
You should ride, Cowboy, ride;

He loaded up his trailer then stopped in at the dance,
She'd done caught his eye, he thought he'd take a chance,
His header cut him off, 'fore he was too far gone,
Said they should be goin,' "it's time to move on;"

Her daddy sold insurance in a nearby town,
She'd been a rodeo queen with a banner and hat crown,
She's been takin' classes at a campus near her home,
He could get a job, settle down, and never roam;

He thought it was love, might even sell his horse,
Then the nonsense hit him with a mighty force,
He might pawn his saddle, he might borrow a rope,
But lettin' go of his horse, he had one word, "Nope;"

He rode into the arena on his great big bay,
The girl in the first box said, "I'll marry him someday,"
Don't think he didn't see her with all of her appeals,
But when he threw that heel loop, he came up with two heels;

# Leavin' Town

There's a big old sorrel gelding waitin' outside by the rail,
He wants to take me outta here and move on down the trail,
But I got some whiskey in me as I step out of the bar,
To take him to the livery, it's not very far;

I climb into the saddle, 'cause I don't walk that much,
Take a pull from my bottle, give my horse a gentle touch,
When he takes off like lightnin' I nearly come uncorked,
I look down at 'im wonderin' whose bronc had I just forked;

He's runnin' leavin' town, as my bottle hits the ground,
I'm clutchin' to the saddle horn, I've got to slow him down,
That gelding runs up a ridge, and slows down near the top,
I gather up my reins and finally bring him to a stop;

I pull his head back to me then take a good deep breath,
Knowin' ever inch of me had barely escaped death,
Lookin' back there's people standin,' laughin' in the street,
My pride is fairly bruised, well, there's other folks to meet;

I give that sorrel his head, he quickly shows them folks his tail,
We're both pretty eager to move on down the trail,
Now, I'm sittin' in another bar, no wait, don't think the worst,
That big old sorrel's bedded down, now that He comes first!

# There's A Cowboy At the Gate

Pa, there's a cowboy at the gate,
DON'T LET HIM IN!
He's wearin' a big old hat and a silly grin,
He says he's got a job he's got to do,
There's a cowboy at the gate,
DON'T LET HIM THROUGH!

He says that he met sister at the dance,
He thought he'd ride up here and take a chance,
He's picked her flowers and he hopes to talk to you,
There's a cowboy at the gate,
DON'T LET HIM THROUGH!

But sister's seen him waitin' at the gate,
She's hopin' you'll let them go on a date,
'Cause all the boys she knows, well they're all kin,
There's a cowboy at the gate,
DON'T LET HIM IN!

Ma comes in and says, "Don't be afraid,"
You don't want her to become an old maid,
Sister's behind Ma, sayin,' "Daddy, PLEASE,"
There's a cowboy at the gate,
SEND HIM TO ME!

# Nylon Ropes and Barb Wire

I sure miss the brandin' fire,
Nylon ropes and barb wire,
Shaps and spurs and burnin' hair,
Cold, clear springs and mountain air;

Brandin' irons and piggin' strings,
Seein' what the mornin' brings,
Sandstone bluffs, big tall pines,
Wild grapes and columbines;

If I could, I'd go back,
Catch my mule, load my pack,
Ride old trails and make dry camp,
Write a letter by a coal oil lamp;

Yeah, I miss workin' cows,
Doin' as much as time allows,
Grandpa showin' us a better trail,
Rattlesnakes and fools' quail;

The dogs barkin' a lion's treed,
Horsehair headstall, cotton lead,
Roughout boots and batwing shaps,
Chuck boxes and curb straps;

Coyotes yippin' at the break of day,
I even miss haulin' hay,
I miss brother showin' me how,
To get around and turn a cow;

Grassy meadows, McKenna Park,
Blue jays and the meadow lark,
Box canyons you can't get through,
Mountain peaks and skies of blue;

Coffee pot on a Sibley stove,
Old oak trees and an aspen grove,
Prince Albert in a can,
The smell of bacon in a fryin' pan;

Wooden matches and a brandin' box,
Bobcats and the sly old fox,
Biscuits made in a flour sack,
A great big deer, did you see his track;

Yeah, I miss the brandin' fire,
Nylon ropes and barb wire,
Chaps and spurs and burnin' hair,
Cold, clear springs and mountain air;

# Wranglin' the Horses

We was up before daybreak, you could just barely see,
'Cause wranglin' the horses was up to brother and me,
We'd walk out the pasture, where'd them durned horses hide,
With three horses each, we'd have a fresh one to ride;

They'd hid 'neath the trees in a canyon below,
When they topped out, to the corral they would go,
"Dynamite" was usually out in the lead,
They knew where to go so we'd bring 'em some feed;

Oats in morrals, then scatter their hay,
No time to think of the rest of the day,
Walk to the cabin, wash up, breakfast's done,
Then washin' them dishes was never no fun;

Catch your horse, brush him off, then get him saddled,
Get on quick, don't let him know that you're rattled,
At the horse pasture gate I'd try to be last,
If I had to get off, I'd get back on fast;

More'n one good cowboy took a wild ride there,
We acted wild and woolly, like we just didn't care,
But ever' one knew we had respect for out horse,
"Turn loose of that horn," was answered, "Of course;"

We'd gather and brand, them days sure were long,
Pack water, split wood, 'til the day was plumb gone,
Then we's up before daybreak, you could just barely see,
'Cause wranglin' the horses was up to brother and me.

# There's A Place In Heaven (for a cowboy)

There's a place in heaven for a cowboy,
A cowboy who's worked his whole life long,
There's a place in heaven for a cowboy,
Whose heart's out on the range where it belongs;

The Lord will surely smile on a cowboy,
As he leads his horse through the Pearly Gate,
There'll be old friends waitin' for a cowboy,
To tell him his rewards are great;

There's a place in heaven for a cowboy,
A cowboy who did his best down here,
There's a place in heaven for a cowboy,
A cowboy who roped his final steer;

I know The Lord will smile on a cowboy,
As he rides up to the "Big House" on High,
There'll be some "funnin'" waitin' for a cowboy,
As he walks up to the bunkhouse in the sky;

There's a place in heaven for a cowboy,
A cowboy who's worked his whole life long,
There's a place in heaven for a cowboy,
Whose heart's out on the range where it belongs.

# Snowy Visit

We'd been workin' out of the line-camp,
the last day we's done by noon,
Jim said, "We'll be back to the main ranch,
'fore dark, if we leave real soon;"

I told 'em, "I'm tired of this weather,"
last few days, we'd seen plenty of snow,
I saw Bob already grinnin,'
I told 'em, "Get your gear, let's go;"

Jim asked, "Do we take out our bedrolls,"
I said, "No, we'll be back next week,"
Bob said, "We can stop by the Campbell's,"
"It's not far off the trail to the creek;"

The Campbells were neighborin' ranchers,
Ol' Jake was a heck of a man,
We all thought the world of our neighbor,
I told 'em, "We'll stop if we can;"

Wasn't long 'fore them boys was mounted,
Soon we's at the horse pasture gate,
We's glad to be headin' down country,
'Though we knew that we'd get in late;

We's puttin' the miles behind us,
Winter days so quickly turn night,
We's glad when the moon a-risin,'
Was a big old moon, full and bright;

They's grinnin' when I turned to the Campbell's,
They knew that they would get fed,
Or, at least, they'd be some hot coffee,
At the Campbell's warm ranchhouse ahead;

Ol' Jake was out at the woodpile,
When the three of us cowboys rode up,
He said, "Put your mounts in the barn, boys,"
I said, "We only have time for a cup;"

He said, "There's plenty of coffee,"
"I's just takin' a little wood in,"
Bob and Jim already had armloads,
Jake could do nothin,' but grin;

We all hauled wood to the ranchhouse,
It was warm and real cozy in there,
The smell of bread in the oven,
Filled the house with some mighty fine air;

We hung our hats and coats near the fire,
Took a minute so we could get warm,
Mrs. Campbell said, "Here's you some coffee,"
Bob said, "That won't do no harm;"

The kids brought us out some cookies,
I said, "We don't mean to bother you none,"
Jake said, "You boys, are never a bother,"
"Havin' visitors is always good fun;"

Well, we stayed and talked more than I planned on,
And rode home by the light of the moon,
We had a warm feelin' inside us,
We won't forget that visit soon.

# Old Wizard

Workin' cows in the mountains, I's ridin' "Old Wizard,"
I had to stay awake, he'd spook at a lizard,
I's pushin' cows down a ridge from up high,
When I forgot and got to lookin' up at the sky;

Yeah, you see it comin' but my mind was plumb gone,
I couldn't have told you what horse I was on,
They's a big puffy cloud like a huge butter churn,
When he jumped I passed the point of no return;

I grabbed for the horn but caught nothin' but air,
Then, for eternity, I just floated out there,
I'm sure I's a sight, I'd lost all my grace,
With pure surprised fear all over my face;

I hit the ground like I'd been hit by a truck,
"Old Wizard" had just jumped, he didn't even buck,
I laid there a minute to make sure I weren't broke,
Then, right behind me, the trail boss spoke;

Snickerin,' he asked, "Are you takin' a break,"
Smart-like I answered, "No, I'm trailin' a snake,"
He caught up "Old Wizard," then we moved them cows out,
I'll catch hell in the bunkhouse tonight, there's no doubt.

# Granny's Roof

I'm standin' in the pasture wishin' it would rain,
Then the grass would grow so the cows would gain,
As I'm mendin' fence I look across the flat,
I'm out here workin' but where is my mind at;

I'm thinkin' of a time when the sun didn't scorch,
Listenin' to the rain out on Granny's porch,
It can rain on the Gila and I have the proof,
The sound of rain on Granny's old tin roof;

Granny's in her kitchen, chicken 'n dumplin's cookin,'
Grandpa's down the road, he just went lookin,'
It's rainin' up Bear Creek, it's rainin' on Spar,
It's rainin' on the ranch where my memories are;

I'm back in my old truck, today's fence mendin's done,
Headin' back to the house, watchin' the settin' sun,
I know this drought will end like all the others have,
Wait, that two year old is down, bet she's tryin' to calve;

Looks like I won't get home soon, like I planned to do,
That's okay I'm ranchin' like I always wanted to,
'Though the work and worry never seem to end,
I'll think of rain on Granny's roof, the roof I have to mend.

# A Cowboy's Savior

Lord, I'm sittin' here twirlin' my rope,
That smell, you smell is my saddle soap,
I need Your help 'cross this slippery slope,
I'm down on my luck and mighty thin on hope;

I know I bring bad luck down on myself,
Like that "Huck Finn" book up on my shelf,
Next to the "Good Book" with Your Holy Word,
I feel close to you when I'm ridin' herd;

Thank You for this life You blessed me with,
'Though I don't live up to the "Cowboy" myth,
You can't live high on what a cowboy earns,
But you can fill volumes with what a cowboy learns;

I've gone down plenty of them wrong trails,
Wound up in a couple of county jails,
You know I backed up and made a fresh start,
'Cause You sent my angels and they've got my heart;

If ever a cowboy needed a reason to walk tall,
You gave me the best reasons ever come to call,
My kids, the best kids any man ever had,
Showed me how to get over bein' hurt and mad;

You know Your angels have my heart, my love,
At times, I wonder what am I thinkin' of,
How can these angels have such love for me,
But I have faith in You, Lord, all's as it should be;

Well, thank You, Lord, I feel better now,
Like a baby calf that found its' lost cow,
A good talk with You makes my worries lighter,
A good talk with my angels makes my day brighter.

# Cowboys' Mornin'

When it's early in the mornin' and you hear an old cow bawl,
With a coyote yippin' somewhere and a big elk's bugle call,
As you walk out of the bunkhouse the sun ain't come up yet,
You head down to the barn, them chores ain't done themselves, I bet;

You fork hay up in the manger, feed the beeves a little corn,
Put oats out to the horses, check the calf so recent born,
As you're walkin' to the cookshack, you see some signs of dawn,
You smell the bacon fryin' and you know they's coffee on;

That's when you really know how great a life you chose,
As the early sounds hit your ears and bacon strikes your nose,
You wash up in cool water from a pan outside the door,
Then scrape your dirty boots 'cause Pete's just swept the floor;

All the early mornin' cowboys are in high spirits now,
They're all glad to be here, they thank Pete for the chow,
Then they head to the corral to catch their mornin' ride,
Pete just says, "Be careful" then heads right back inside;

The crew will laugh and joke as they head off down the trail,
Pickin' on the last man, they call him "the old cow's tail,"
But when it comes to workin' they work harder than they joke,
Makin' a hand on any horse, even if he's just half broke;

You're mighty glad to be here workin' with this crew,
Doin' what you want, not just what you have to do,
Nowhere is there a better life than bein' a cowhand,
In the early cowboy mornin,' a'ridin' for the brand.

# Turnin' Out the Grey

I won't forget the sight we found that day,
Jim was tryin' to get home, he's ridin' his grey,
In stormy weather lightnin' struck from the sky,
Don't know why Jim and his grey had to die;

We buried 'em on the hill, beyond the corral,
Jim and his grey that he liked so well,
Then strange things began happenin' here,
Ben's horse kicked him behind his left ear;

We thought, for days, Ben'd wind up dead,
Doc come to see him, he's a week in bed,
He got to mixin' up his past and future tense,
'Times he'd tell stories that didn't make sense;

One night, he couldn't sleep, so I stayed up with him,
'Said he'd seen that grey horse and he'd seen Jim,
I tried to comfort him, but it was gettin' late,
He said, "Jim's turnin' out the grey through a big, shiny gate;"

I sat there, listenin,' didn't know what to say,
"A wrangler, named Pete, told Jim, 'That's a mighty fine grey,'"
"But you come in, Jim, the gate's open to you,"
Jim said, "I'm just here to put the grey through;"

Pete said, "Let's talk to The Boss, He's waitin' for you,"
"There's horses to care for, and plenty to do,"
Jim laughed and said, "Sure, I reckon I'll stay,"
"But I's only here to turn out the grey;"

Soon Ben fell asleep and I took a long walk,
When Ben got better, he didn't remember that talk,
I'm sure that wrangler was Saint Peter, up above,
And Jim's tendin' them horses with pure cowboy love;

No doubt Jim's thoughts were just about the grey,
Gettin' him out to pasture, then Jim'd go away,
Feels good knowin' there's cowboys and horses up there,
And a power watchin' over us with heavenly care.

# The Textin' Cowboy

I'm the textin'est cowboy that ever did ride,
These open plains 'neath skies big and wide,
So when I jumped a big steer, sent a txt to big bro,
"jmpd big str, up rdge, hre we go:"

Well, I didn't know that my service was bad,
I didn't know one bar's all I had,
I didn't know my txt didn't arrive,
When I sent: "trnd hm west, all stll alive;"

Turned him down a canyon, back t'ward the herd,
Bro had to be ready, so I sent the word,
"cmin 2 ya, at a fst lpe,"
"keep u I's opn, tke dwn Ur rpe;"

The steer crossed a ridge and ran down a hill,
Hit brother's horse and caused a big spill,
When the dust settled, bro's mad as a hornet,
He took my phone from me, and busted it, darnit;

Now that steer's gone to Texas, I'm usin' "snail mail,"
And yes, there's a moral to this little tale,
Don't assume communication's has always got through,
'Cause I'm shoveling out corrals, wanna join me, do you;

# Between the Doors

I rode up the hill to church today
to say one last "goodbye,"
To a friend too soon removed from us
I sit and wonder why,
So many people we care for
are gone before their time,
Suddenly they're gone from us
just as they reach their prime;

I rode up the hill to church today
feelin' quite remote,
Thinkin' of the life that's gone
my heart was in my throat,
It's my misfortune that I mourn
I should have visited more,
So now I've come to witness
the closing of a door;

The door is only open at birth
then again at death,
We live between the doors
as we draw each mortal breath,
We think we have an idea of
what lies beyond the doors,
But how on earth can we imagine
those near, yet fleeting shores;

I rode up the hill to church today
to say one last "Goodbye."

#

I cut a two track road down to my lower fence,
To a homestead, long abandoned, seemed no one's been there since,
I took a break in the shade beneath an old oak tree,
Drank a beer on my tailgate, thinkin' 'bout ranch history;

On the ground were rusted buggy springs, and parts of it's brake,
Then branches started swayin' and oak leaves began to shake,
A circle of shimmerin' light seemed to float in the air,
Through the circle, the oak looked smaller, and a horse was tied up there;

A black "spring buggy" beyond the oak, looked almost new,
A man shoein' the horse saw me, then he dropped the shoe,
He reminded me of "Granny" he waved, I said, "Hi,"
We couldn't hear each other, but he looked me in the eye;

He saw my orange Chevy and motioned four times four,
I laughed and mimed, "four wheel drive," then opened up a door,
I reached in my cooler and got an ice cold beer,
Handed it, and a new dollar through the window, tremblin' with fear;


He reached out and took them I motioned to twist the top,
He read the date on the bill, I watched his chin drop,
He motioned that over there it was nineteen and twenty three,
As the "window" began to fade, he drew an "X" beneath the tree;

I got my shovel from my truck and dug where he made the mark,
Found a metal box he'd buried, it was rusty, damp, and dark,
A tintype of his family, and a gold eagle from the Denver Mint,
A distant uncle, but to explain it, I just don't have a hint.

# The Sun Comes Up Each Mornin'

The sun comes up each mornin'
such a sight to see,
Go fill your coffee cups
then come sit here with me,
There's stories I'd like to share
but there's plans we need to make,
Cattle that need gatherin'
and "rained-on" hay to rake;

I'll go run the tractor, girls
you take the crew and ride,
Push them cows to the corral
and put 'em all inside,
I'll come up and help you'all
to get the brandin' done,
The hay won't dry enough to bale
'til we see another sun;

But the sun comes up each mornin'
with so much work to do,
If we could hire two more hands
we'd have a full size crew,
Tomorrow we'll be haulin' hay
we'll stack it in the barn,
And if we had more time, sweet daughters,
I'd tell you one more yarn.

# My Talkin' Horse

I's ridin' my bay gelding high on Tadpole Ridge,
I couldn't get him to go beneath a natural bridge,
He balked and he snorted, he said he wouldn't go,
Well, he didn't tell me, but he let me know;

I tried to skirt around it but there was just no way,
When I begged and pleaded, he said, "Not today,"
Finally, I tricked him to go beneath the rock,
Man, he would have cussed me if he just could talk;

I backed him halfway through, then turned him twice around,
That was one mad gelding, kickin' at the ground,
As we went beneath that bridge, the sky all turned black,
My horse looked at me and said, "We should just go back;"

I know I'm sorta stubborn and 'times I play the fool,
My horse says that sometimes I act like a mule,
While we kept on movin' I looked up at the sky,
I saw three moons up there, that's when I said, "Goodbye;"

That bay horse spun around, we loped back through the bridge,
I learned another lesson way up on Tadpole Ridge,
Listen to your horse when he's takin' care of you,
'Cause he'll sense the danger, long before you do.

# Circlin'

We had to change the leathers on the windmill up the creek,
And the old rusty standpipe had sprung another leak,
I take the pickup with the tools loaded in the back,
The new hand takes the tractor, he'll stay in my track;

I get to the windmill late, had a flat along the way,
Thinkin' I should put this off until a better day,
But the wind hasn't started yet so I pull the windmills' brake,
The tail starts in but it's more than the cable can take;

The cable snaps and bangs the tower as it's fallin' down,
Standin' behind the pickup, man, I like it on the ground,
I grab a chain and climb up, I'll tie it off real soon,
I hear the tractor comin,' the new hand's whistlin' a happy tune;

I grab the tail to tie the chain so it won't come loose,
A gust of wind spins the fan and I take off like a goose,
I got ahold of the tail so I climb up on top,
The tractor comes up to the mill, by now the whistlin's stopped;

I tell myself, "I'm saved" this guy might make a real good Pard,
But when he tries to stop, he slams the right brake way too hard,
The brake hangs up, he's circlin' and he don't know what to do,
The wind is really whippin' now and I start circlin,' too;

The crows all leave the country 'cause we're circlin' too much here,
As we're both a-hollerin' we learn some about fear,
I'm wishin' I could grow wings, so I could just take flight,
The new hand on the tractor just keeps circlin' to the right;

Later that old tractor finally runs plumb out of gas,
I get off the mill as it makes a real slow pass,
We pull up to the toolshed at the days' last light,
The foreman stops us, sayin,' "You'll finish tomorrow, right;"

# Horseshoe Pasture

There is a place back in the hills that takes my breath away,
Old adobe house, now fallin' down, was nice back in its' day,
Tall sandstone bluffs line the valley where the cabin lies,
Here you can sit by an old pine tree watchin' an eagle as it flies;

The windmill turns and pumps fresh water that tastes almost sweet,
Into a tank where we can swim escapin' the summer's heat,
The old corral don't need much work to hold a bunch of cattle,
Right near the gate a palomino uncorked me from my saddle;

The Horseshoe Pasture with its' tall oaks, juniper, and pine,
Tugs at my heart with some of the fondest memories of mine,
The winter I ran a trapline, caught my first coyote here,
Brought more work than payoff, that cold and snowy year;

I remember cuttin' a Christmas tree, on the road above the bluff,
With my grandparents in the old jeep, that road's still mighty rough,
It snowed all mornin' then the sun came out, shinin' fresh and bright,
Bouncin' off the brand new snow like tiny silver lights;

There's nothin' in the world that makes me feel so young and free,
As bein' in that valley when my family's there with me,
We may cut wood, take a swim, or just enjoy the day,
See, there's still a place, back in the hills, that takes my breath away.

# Where I Belong

The snow wants to blow in New Mexico
Man, it sure is cold,
The breeze makes the trees start to freeze
This is gettin' old,
The horses turn their tails to the wind,
This cabin's cold as it's ever been,
As my patience starts to grow thin,
The fire starts burnin' strong,
And I'm where I belong;

The moanin' and groanin' of the wind
reach my sleepin' ears,
Old faces and places I've been
fade as the mornin' nears,
The horses are doin' all right,
It quit snowin' sometime durin' the night,
The world is covered in white,
And there is nothin' wrong,
'Cause I'm where I belong;

I need to read a Zane Grey
take a day of rest,
But I must go bust ice today
every day's a test,
The horses, like me, don't want to go,
Ridin' in the frozen snow,
At least the wind has ceased to blow,
So I sing my favorite song,
As I ride along,
'Cause I'm right where I belong.

# I Keep My Feet On The Ground

Sometimes the wind will blow too much,
Sometimes the ground's too hot to touch,
Sometimes my baby's too far away,
But I'm here workin' for another day;

The rain keeps fallin,' the wind keeps blowin,'
The world keeps turnin' around,
The sun keeps shinin,' I look for silver linin's,
While I keep my feet on the ground;

The days keep passin,' though they're too long,
Beside my baby's where I belong,
I'll be here workin' for some time to come,
Then back to my baby, I'll make my run;

The rain keeps fallin,' the wind keeps blowin,'
The world keeps turnin' around,
The sun keeps shinin,' I look for silver linin's,
While I keep my feet on the ground;

The pay's too short, the hours never end,
Money seems to go blowin' in the wind,
I keep thinkin' somethin's gonna change,
But this cowboy's still ridin' the range;

The rain keeps fallin,' the wind keeps blowin,'
The world keeps turnin' around,
The sun keeps shinin,' I look for silver linin's,
While I keep my feet on the ground;

# Shorty's Dream

I got up early that mornin,' wrangled horses to the pen,
If I'd a' seen the trouble comin,' I'd a' scattered 'em to the wind,
But ever'thing was normal, it was just another day,
I corralled and grained the horses then threw them out some hay;

I walked down to the cabin for my halter and some grub,
Old Shorty was plumb surly, like a sow bear that lost her cub,
But his bacon and biscuits was good, he was a real good cook,
As I filled my coffee cup, I asked what had him shook;

He grumbled then he told me, he'd had a bad nightmare,
He'd jumped awake from fallin' off a bluff way up there,
I looked where he pointed, the ridge we planned to work that day,
I said, "Let's work Stone Canyon, clean Dog Springs along our way;"

Well, Shorty got indignant, said, "Hell, it's just a dream,"
We saddled up and rimmed out the trail above the stream,
We gathered on the North Side, crossed the ridge with all them cows,
Lined 'em down the rimrock trail, single file's all it allows;

In a narrow spot, I's ahead, Shorty's ridin' behind me,
I heard steel grate on slickrock, I looked back in time to see,
Shorty's horse had fallen sendin' Shorty over the edge,
When I got there he's forty feet down, layin' on a ledge;

I got our ropes and climbed down, it was done too late,
I guess his dream foretold this, or did it seal his fate,
I wish I'd done something, I could have made a change,
Now his grave's behind the cabin, way out there on the range.

# One Last Request

When my last ride here is done,
And I've followed the settin' sun,
Hope the memories are mostly good,
One last request, if I could;

Put my boots down near my feet,
Put my hat in there with me,
My pocket knife, don't forget that,
And know I'm smilin' where I'm at;

God kept my sorrel for the day,
I get back to my cowboy way,
I'll be followin' some old cow's tail,
Down some old familiar trail;

This afterlife may be a dream,
Like drinkin' from a mountain stream,
I hope to gather cows on High,
While ridin' herd up in the sky;

That's my vision so let it be,
Now close your eyes and maybe see,
That my vision may be right,
We're pushin' God's herd toward the light;

So, put my boots down near my feet,
Put my hat in there with me,
My pocketknife, don't forget that,
Then know I'm smilin' where I'm at.

# Ridin' the Outlaw Zones

I didn't choose this life, somehow it chose me,
Livin' high and wild sometimes can get lonely,
There's a girl I dream of but she's way back home,
Someday I'd like to settle down, then I'd never roam;

(chorus:)
Ridin' the outlaw zones and livin' in nameless dreams,
This is the life I live, I accept what it means,
Carin' for my horses, makin' sure they can run,
I keep my holsters oiled and daily clean my guns;

Sometimes I work on ranches, I like workin' cattle,
I'm sure that I'll die in a saloon or in my saddle,
At times I get caught out, then I make dry camp,
She is always in the dreams of this saddle tramp;

Sure would like to settle down, raise some cows someplace,
Takin' care of business, watchin' her pretty face,
Don't think that it's possible with this life I lead,
Knowin' ever' day what I want and what I need;

I ride into the little town and meet the marshal's eyes,
That he knows who I am comes as no surprise,
I step down at the grocer's and get just what I must,
How can I settle down if I'm always buildin' dust;

I'm really gettin' tired of the outlaw trail,
Knowin' how it all will end, if I ever fail,
It'll all be over if I'm too slow on the draw,
But she's always in the dreams of an old outlaw;

# Mesilla Night

I was stayin' in Mesilla, workin' not too far away,
It was up 'fore light and ride out as we watched the breakin' day,
We worked the boss's cattle out west of the Rio Grande,
On friday nights we'd dance to a mariachi band;

I was dancin' to a cumbia with a gorgeous brown eyed girl,
Watchin' her eyes sparkle and her long black hair twirl,
We slow danced together and I held her close to me,
I asked if I could call on her, she quickly answered, "Si;"

(chorus:)
We walked out in the plaza holding hands beneath the stars,
Soft music came down narrow streets from the local bars,
When her friend turned away, to my great surprise,
She reached up and kissed me, love sparkling in her eyes;

It was bittersweet to watch her leave as the night came to an end,
Weeks later I read the note my love was forced to send,
If I kept calling on her, she'd be sent away,
Out to California, near some town called "San Jose;"

I answered I was going, there's no need to leave her home,
Then I rode out of Mesilla, there were lonely hills to roam,
I wondered how it could have been with her in my life,
Walking through the plaza with my gorgeous, loving wife;

(repeat chorus)

I rode silent trails from Mogollon to Santa Fe,
Did all I could do to make her memory fade away,
Ridin' in the high country, her face was everywhere,
Knowin' that I loved her, I'd repeat, "I just don't care;"

I know she's forgotten me, she's fallen for someone,
I'm out workin' cattle where the bear and wild deer run,
But in the wind I hear mariachis playing soft and light,
The stars are shining like her eyes on that Mesilla night;
(when . . .)
(repeat chorus)

#

The tall pine tree grows stately near the bottom of the creek,
Unlike the older pine tree growin' gnarled up near the peak,
The older tree is twisted and lashed at by the wind,
While in the creek the young tree grows without a single bend;

Now half-way up the rocky slope grows yet another tree,
It seems the tree up on the slope grows happy as can be,
Not cooped up in the bottom with no way to look around,
Not wind blown way up on the ridge with branches on the ground;

It's strange to think what chance means and what our fate bestows,
Wild bunchgrass on the mesa or corn growin' in straight rows,
We can disagree on things, I know that is true,
'Though I like that tree up on the slope, it may not be the one for you.

# Bringin' In a Dogie

I was ridin' in the pasture when I saw a cow was down,
Several cows were close by, millin' all around,
That's when I saw the dogie standin' all alone,
Lookin' at his momma, she was cold as stone;

(Chorus:)
I was bringin' in a dogie, his momma lost her fight,
Bringin' in a dogie, to a future warm and bright,
I was bringin' in a dogie, he would get well fed,
Bringin' in a dogie, to a safe, warm bed;

It was too late for his momma but I had to save that calf,
I snaked a loop around 'im, his fightin' made me laugh,
I set 'im 'cross my saddle then climbed up on my bay,
This wasn't his first dogie, nor his last, no way;

'Fore we got back to headquarters, it started rainin' light,
I wondered if that dogie woulda' made it through the night,
The coyotes coulda' got 'im or he'd a' been a lion kill,
He was partly in my slicker, layin' mighty still;

Dave met me at the barn when I first rode in,
Sara said, "I'll make a bottle," then she was gone, again,
As I brushed my horse down, Dave put the dogie in a stall,
He won't be the last dogie, but we'll try to save 'em all;

# Remember Me, Boys

Remember me, boys when my time has come,
Though my life didn't add up highly as some,
Never got my ranch, I just run a few cows,
But I am as happy as God ever allows;

Had me a wife and I raised up them girls,
Prettiest things that ever wore curls,
Got a big brother who'll be there for me,
And the best big sister there ever could be;

Got me a girl, now, and she's got my heart,
I'll spend more time with her before I depart,
And I'll always know that when I got the chance,
I grabbed life by the tail and I sure as hell danced;

If "Roanie" were to stumble and fall off a bluff,
Don't feel sorry for me, boys, I've lived enough,
Pack me up a ridge, dig a hole deep and long,
Roll me in my blanket, put me where I belong;

Plant me near the trail, boys, way up there on top,
Where a cowboy naturally comes to a stop,
Where he'd rest his horse 'fore he went on his way,
And he might glance down at the grave where I lay;

So, remember me, boys, when my time has come,
Though my life didn't add up highly as some,
Remember that whenever I got the chance,
I grabbed life by the tail, boys, and I sure as hell danced.

Made in the USA
Lexington, KY
12 July 2019